MW01503133

The Road to Phrygia

Louis Garafalo

Outskirts Press, Inc.
Denver, Colorado

This is a work of fiction. The events and characters described here are imaginary and are not intended to refer to specific places or living persons. The opinions expressed in this manuscript are solely the opinions of the author and do not represent the opinions or thoughts of the publisher.

The Road to Phrygia
All Rights Reserved

Copyright © 2007 Louis Garafalo
v2.0

This book may not be reproduced, transmitted, or stored in whole or in part by any means, including graphic, electronic, or mechanical without the express written consent of the publisher except in the case of brief quotations embodied in critical articles and reviews.

Outskirts Press
http://www.outskirtspress.com

ISBN-10: 1-4327-0447-8
ISBN-13: 978-1-4327-0447-6

Outskirts Press and the "OP" logo are trademarks belonging to Outskirts Press, Inc.

Printed in the United States of America

CHAPTER 1

The wind rose up now across the shallow valley, swirling, pushing the soft gray mist into his face and he strained to see the tiny figures on the other side. He pulled at the corner of his hood looking for a dry spot but found everything moist, the mist forming a dewy covering and mixing with the stains of his sweat. His eyes stung, desperate for relief, and yet he could not turn their attention away from the scene below. Squinting, he could make out their forms, only a few left, huddled, the last of the soldiers trudging away from them down the narrow slope. He saw her clearly now, her streaked gray hair, kneeling in the dirt, brushing, smoothing, grasping the hand, raising it to her cheek. After a long moment she rose to her feet, James at her elbow and Mary Magdalene with her hand. They stood linked and slowly turned to watch as three of the men carefully lifted the shrouded body. After a few brief words the men began trailing Joseph down the hill. Then they followed, the last to leave.

Head low, Peter continued to stare at the now empty scene. He backed himself off of the stony ridge line and wedged himself between a large grey boulder and its mossy companion. The wind had picked up, driving its fine sleet forward, all quiet now but for its low, subtle sounds. Peter laid back, beyond exhausted, his eyes inflamed. He pulled back his sweaty hood, tilted his head upward and closed his eyes as the rain fell on his face and his matted hair.

CHAPTER 2

The last were leaving, friends, acquaintances of Joseph's, those that had recently met Mary, neighbors. Mary Magdalene tidied up the tray of cups as James stood at the door and accepted their final condolences. Joseph stood against the wall, surveyed the scene, satisfied, a silent nod to her as he slipped out a side doorway. Then there was silence, the tender warmth within the room slipping out with the departure of the last guest. James closed the wooden door, turned to his mother and met her gaze, saw the sorrowful blankness in her eyes and instinctively rushed to embrace her. She took a responding step and sagged against him. For moments they said nothing, their eyes bitter, welling, their throats tightened and coarse. Mary moved first, pushed away slightly, stared into the eyes of her beloved youngest child, grasped his bearded cheeks with her hands and gently pulled his face to her chest. His tears flowed freely now and his head jerked ever slightly as he tried to regain control. His head still bowed, he choked out, "Mother" and Mary lifted his face.

"My darling child… my darling James."

Mary Magdalene joined them now and they made way for her to enter their embrace. More moments passed. Mary Magdalene spoke first.

"What will you do Mary?"

Mary arched back from their grasp, her head and shoulders following. She looked at them alternately and began to gently shake her head.

"I will finish our business here and return to our home... my home, your father's home...." She inhaled deeply and let out a long slow breath, "... his home."

A jolt of recognition bit through her, an instant of fear, as she looked at James.

"The authorities. James!"

With softened fists he clenched both of her arms, loosely, tenderly.

"Mother, I was there all afternoon. They could have taken me at any time. You as well."

Mary realized that her son was right and she exhaled a long, slow sigh.

"What of the others? What of Peter?"

"I have not seen Peter since last night. The authorities were approaching him. He may be in custody although I think we would have heard about it. Probably in hiding. The others have scattered. Joseph had arranged another meeting place for us, the house of a friend. A bit of a walk, on the other side of the hills. Mary and I will go there tonight and wait for the others. Hopefully, some of them will find their way there. I believe it will be safe."

James realized that he still had hold of his mother's arms and he released his grip. He looked up, looked past her.

"You should come with us."

Mary glanced around the room, feeling the day's exhaustion, her senses beginning to shut down. She could handle no more.

"No, you go. My place is here. I need to attend to some things tomorrow with Joseph... You're right, we are safe, at least for the time being. You need to be with the others. Find them... They must be very afraid."

She pushed her hands together and pressed them against her upper lip and nose, pondering... prayerful.

"It is safe here. They will not bother a grieving mother. Joseph's neighbors are trustworthy.... Tell them to come here and they can then make their escape."

Mary began scooping up pieces of the bread and fruit that had been left by the neighbors and placed them on a tray. She went back to the small kitchen area and found two empty water jars plus a container of wine.

"Take these."

Mary Magdalene grasped the tray and spun it out to her side as she reached to hug Mary with her other arm. Their heads met softly. Mary closed her eyes, reached behind her neck, and gently pulled her closer. Now James approached his mother and put his hands to the side of her head. He pulled her close and buried his face in her graying hair, breathing in deeply. He held his grip, his eyes moistening, his throat instinctively convulsing. Her eyes met his, watery, pink and filmy, yet she spoke in a clear and controlled voice.

"Be well, my darling... My darling James... Be strong... for them... and for your brother. He did love you so."

Mary let out a throaty exhale and James released his grip.

"I love you Mother... I will be careful. I will find who I can find and let them know that they can come here... I am sure that most of them would want to see you."

He positioned the wine jar in front of his chest and grasped the two empty jars with his other hand. Mary Magdalene gave a final glance, a tight, painful smile, and was out the door. James followed but stopped at the threshold.

"If you see Peter, tell him to either stay here or make his way to Joseph's other place. I will be back tomorrow, probably by mid-day."

Mary watched him disappear into the shadows, the night's coolness blowing softly in through the door, a welcome comfort. She made her way across the room and slumped into a chair. She found the wine glass that had been hers and sipped. On the table were the remains of some bread and she dipped the pieces into the dish of honey that had been put out. It was the first she had eaten all day and only then that she noticed that her hands were still dirty from the day's activities. She went over to the washing table, dipped her hands into the basin, and began rubbing. It started as the faintest tint and then turned a full shade of pink. Not dirt but blood. His blood, her son's blood, the reinforcement of the day's awful events. She joined her hands, scooped up a full handful and forcefully spread it over her face trying to somehow reconnect with him. Again and again, her face now dripping and her hairline wringed with wetness. Could it all have really happened? Could this not have been some kind of terrible dream, a terrible disconnection within her imagination?

She looked down at her garments, saw the caked blood, the various stains, pink, wine colored, dark brown. His blood. The awful reminders of the day. The tears came hard now and she gasped, a guttural moan, felt for her bed, and laid herself gently down. She felt the silence, her eyes awash, stark images of the day returning, saw his face again, his last face, and reached out to touch his imaginary hand.

CHAPTER 3

He approached cautiously, his eyes searching again for some hidden guards. He had made a wide sweep in from the sloping hills and had had a continuous view of the site for some time. To his surprise he had seen no one. No guards, no disciples, no curiosity seekers. The night air was very still, cool, crisp… cleansing. Large gray clouds floated past the moon interrupting its light with alternating shadows. He feared exposing himself but he had reached the end of the rocky camouflage. The stone was clearly in view. Taking one final look towards the peripheries, Peter rose up from behind the last rock, paused a moment, then entered the open ground. Some of the clouds skidded past the moon lighting up much of the opening where Peter stood. He felt strangely bemused — was he somehow being purposely exposed? He waited a second moment then proceeded towards the stone. As he neared the stone he could see the opening of the tomb just to the right and slightly uphill from where the stone lay. Strange, he thought, that the guards would not have completed the sealing. He had seen them leave with Joseph and the attendants, probably five or six soldiers, certainly enough men to have rolled the stone in front of the tomb's opening.

As he neared, he moved first to the stone, put his hands on top of it, at even level with his waist, felt its strength, pushed against its unmoving mass. He held that pose, pushing absently against the stone, his mind beginning to flood with images of the last day's events. He glanced at the tomb, beginning to fear, somehow had a sense that the body had been taken. Then he noticed the deep indentations in front of the tomb. Clearly, the stone had been put in place and had been moved. But by whom? The soldiers? Maybe. And maybe that explains the lack of guards. Where would they have taken the body? Maybe they were concerned about Jesus' prediction that he would rise from the dead? Could it have been Joseph and the disciples? It would have taken at least six of them to move it. Could they have made their way here undetected?

The tomb's opening beckoned him. He had to see if the body was in there and try, somehow, to make peace with his departed friend. Try somehow to explain his fears, his actions, his weaknesses. His emotions flooded him now, heat searing up into the sides of his neck, his tears blurring his vision as he stood next to the opening. He asked forgiveness from his friend, steadied himself, preparing himself for this dreaded viewing. Then he stooped, peered into the opening, squinted for light and angle, saw nothing in the narrow darkness. Hesitating just a moment, he reached inside, full to his shoulders, and extended his hand.

He could feel nothing.

Peter pulled back from the tomb, took the several steps back to the stone, braced his back against it, and slid to his seat. He stared straight ahead, his mind swirling and yet strangely blank. His thoughts filled with images of the past days' events alternately clear and focused; dim and fleeting. They flooded him, overwhelmed his senses, disjointed memories, out of sequence, out of control, beyond his understanding now. He tried to focus, straining for logic. Why was the body not here? What could have happened to it? Who would have had access to it? To this site? Was it even taken here? Had Joseph made other arrangements? Had Mary or James requested some sort of change? Worried, perhaps, about a desecration? And yet the stone had clearly been in place and had clearly been moved. A grand deception carried out by James and the disciples? Some sort of staged "resurrection"? No, clearly the authorities would not have allowed such a sham. And he had seen all of the soldiers....

How had this all come to happen? Hadn't Jesus' greatest public triumph come just days before? The glorious entry into the city, the excitement, the completion of the journey. Could it have been only days ago? Peter had not known what to expect when Jesus had informed him of their entry into Jerusalem but his anticipations were without limit. Would the heavens actually split? Would Moses himself be there to greet them? A massive uprising perhaps, a triumph so magnificent that the Romans would lay prostrate and silent in recognition, their Caesar impotent and exposed? Peter thought of their last night together, the supper, the huge gathering, the room filled with their warmth, a strange and yet exuberant tension everywhere throughout the room. They had all strained to get near him, drawn towards something, into something, that none of them could define nor resist. Peter had sensed it. James, as well. Philip and Andrew and John, all shooting glances at each other, each feeling — no, knowing — that the hour had come. His hour, their hour. Their work, so righteous and yet so filled with sacrifice, was about to manifest itself, unknowing in form but containing certain glory. Truly their defining moment had come.

Peter fidgeted in the dirt now, his clothing moist, soiled, irritating, as his thoughts returned him to present consciousness. Despite the coolness, Peter was sweating profusely, desperately trying to eject the embarrassment that coursed throughout his body. Here he was, Peter, the "Rock." Even Jesus had called him that on occasion. He had earned that name from them, first through physical strength and later through steadfast determination, silent leadership. Yes, truly he had been their leader. And now, here he was, leaning against a stone. A mere rock, and yet it had guarded his dear friend, had somehow been closer to Jesus than he had allowed himself to be in the hour when men stood up with their friends.

He could not stay still, his shame welling from his heart, pulsing through him, coating his skin. He balled a fist and pressed it hard into his forehead, squinting back his pain. He rose to his feet, wicked his eyebrows, shook off the caked dirt, tried to wipe the sides of his face, one then the other. His failure consumed him, exhausted him, unrelenting, no release. Had it all been so obvious? The glare from Jesus, quick and dark. The nonchalance of his jibe - "You will deny me three times." - Peter's impending failure apparently so visible to the man who had come to mean everything to him. He could recall it all now, sharp in detail. He saw the authorities leading the group away, the pack of soldiers surrounding Jesus, his head pushed down. More soldiers, searching sideways, others of the disciples stopped now, standing, watching the group pull away, only James chasing along, jumping up to see his brother, shouting, yammering. His fear rising as the soldiers approached him, searing when he was identified. Confusion. Where was his strength? Where was the promised power? Weren't they behind him now — angels, chariots, Moses, David himself? The hour was here! Where were they? Where was Jesus? Their triumph?

He caught a last sight of James, saw the group turn the corner, gone, other soldiers now turned directly towards him, fierce, glaring. Then silence.

"You are with him!"

"No."

"You are one of them!"

"No!"

"Come with us!"

"I don't know the man!"

He could replay the scene and hear his own words, clear, penetrating, steely, again and again, relentless, surreal, unmistakably his. It had happened so quickly and yet he had responded with no hesitation. And somehow he had seen it so clearly, this Jesus, this man so magnetic and so powerful who had seen fit to choose Peter as his second. The "Rock" reduced to human clay.

The night air whistled ever faintly now, the moon's light was clear, the clouds seeming to have moved past. In such brightness, he felt his physical exposure acutely and yet he also felt no concern whatsoever. He had so feared discovery over the past two days. But now, discovery would promise relief from aloneness and self-imprisonment.

Peter moved a step towards the tomb, thought of some words he had heard Jesus speak many times, about asking the Father for things in Jesus' name, that such prayers would be heard and never denied. He thought of those words now, words he had so willingly accepted and professed, words which had been far from his consciousness over the past days, words that needed to be re-heard, re-learned, re-believed, re-trusted. New words, old words with new meaning. He turned back to the stone, fell to his knees, raised his hands prayerfully, first to his nose then to his hairline, felt his forehead and hands press against the stone. The first wails began to emerge, silently, internal, then murmurs, slight spasms, then cries, the weight of his failure overwhelming him. He confessed his weakness and his shame, accepted their bitter acknowledgement, and begged the Father for forgiveness, controlled at first then ever louder. He professed his love for Jesus, words he now realized that he had never said to Jesus before. Eyes pressed closed, the words re-emerged and were repeated, their repetition beginning to bring some control back to him. Then silence, self-talk, more silence, the beginning of a faint calm.

Peter took a long, slow breath, exhaled its contents, felt his chest dip slightly as if casting off a weight, his head lurching forward. His eyes had been tightly closed and, as he opened them, he fought to shake their darkness and to regain focus. With their clearing, he realized that he was engulfed in a shadow. He turned to his right looking past the tomb and slightly upward.

He was no longer alone.

CHAPTER 4

Peter lifted his head, looked up towards the figure outlined in front of him, perhaps ten feet away. The figure appeared shadowy at first against the night sky and Peter's eyes instinctively tried to adjust their focus. There was silence and Peter could hear his own quick, short breaths. Tall, covered by a plain white cloak, the familiar hairline and beard wringing the face.

Before him stood Jesus.

Jesus started towards Peter, moved two steps down the slight incline, and was now within arm's length. Peter was immobilized, his lips pursed shut, sticky, shoulders weighted, hands unresponsive, hanging, his emotions blank. He could see the eyes now, darkly brown, intense, the prominent nose, the high cut cheeks, the lips beginning to part.

"Peter, it's me, Jesus... Peace be with you Peter."

Peter heard the words, just above a whisper, the deep tone so familiar yet already distant, buried in memory. He stared at Jesus, met his eyes, the face looking detached as if painted against the black sky. Peter tilted his head slightly, eyes forming a squint, his arms still dangling, hands lifeless. He saw the arm raise, the hand extending from the light garment, the long fingers touching his shoulder, firm, warm, breaking the surreal moment.

"Peter, don't be afraid. It's me... Don't be afraid my friend."

With those words Jesus reached for Peter's other shoulder, clasped and began to lift. Peter felt a rush of consciousness, a strange warmth and energy, and pushed himself to his feet. Jesus kept his grip, moved to the tips of the powerful shoulders, held him at length. Jesus looked deeply into Peter's eyes, some touch of wonder showing, his own eyes beginning to soften, liquid, filling slightly.

"Peter."

Jesus inhaled deeply, saying nothing, and then slowly, steadily released his breath.

Jesus pulled Peter full against himself and Peter, still dazed, could feel the warmth, could smell the manhood, could sense the life force. Incredibly, this was indeed Jesus! Jesus held his grip from behind Peter's shoulders but allowed their two bodies to separate slightly. Again, he looked directly into Peter's eyes and began shaking his head slowly, gently, his eyes warming, his lips parting into the beginnings of a slight, affirming smile. Jesus took in a long breath, held it, then let it out full, almost with relief. His teeth shone brightly now in a full smile. He looked slightly bemused, nearing laughter, joyful. His eyes caught Peter's again.

"Today is the day of days Peter."

Peter heard the words, clear yet dream-like, tried to

swallow, his throat dry, croaking, his thoughts askew, surreal but re-shaping, adrenaline flowing now, his paralysis beginning to evaporate. He stared at Jesus, only inches away, his smile full, his face magnificently radiant. Peter felt a rush, a swift and instant return to the moment, his mind incredibly clear now. He looked into the eyes, recognized Jesus anew, felt his body flash with fear, excitement, the terrible recognition kicking full into his senses. Peter dropped to his knees, then flush to the ground, prostrate, his face resting on the back of his hands.

"My Lord and my God," he murmured, trembling.

Peter could sense the sweat accumulating on his brow and could feel it rolling down the side of his face and behind his ears. His body was in full reaction now to the terrorizing excitement of Jesus' presence and his corresponding sense of naked exposure. Nervously, instinctively, he wiped his hands one against the other, the beads of sweat swirling with the bits of dirt. He realized that he was incredibly foul, his body and clothes reflecting a two-day mixture of perspiration, rain, and mud. He tried again to clean his hands and sensed that Jesus had moved to within an arm's length.

"You are a bit of a mess my friend."

Peter looked up at Jesus, his eyes blank, idle, stinging. He could say nothing.

Jesus reached down and took Peter's hand, rubbing his thumb across the knuckles. The top of Peter's hand was smeared with streaks of watery mud and his pores continued to bead up. Jesus looked away for a second and mumbled something inaudible to Peter. Incredibly, Peter felt the top of his hand tingle and the perspiration begin to bubble up, not beads now but droplets. Jesus tilted Peter's hand downward, bent it at the wrist, and both watched as rivulets rolled towards Peter's fingers cleaning his hand completely. Jesus said nothing. He then took Peter's other hand, tilted it into position, and both watched as the cleansing water rolled off Peter's fingers and onto the ground.

"Water," Jesus said softly.

Peter turned his hands over and felt the same sensation take over the inside of both his palms. Fat drops of water began pulsing through his pores and he instinctively curled his fingers, his indented palms filling. His hands now completely clean, Peter could only stare at them, silent and amazed.

Jesus said nothing, turned and looked away. Peter caught his profile, thought Jesus' eyes looked distant, unfocused, deep in thought. Jesus looked off, as if scanning for a lost star, then raised his arms, clasped his hands at the knuckles, and raised them to his chin. He continued his stare. Then, with his hands still at his chin, Jesus tilted his head towards Peter, his mouth showing the beginning of a wry smile.

"I am not of this world now Peter… and yet I continue in this world."

His eyes caught Peter's and Peter could see the change, Jesus' eyes snapping into focus, sharp now, immediate and present. A full minute passed in silence.

"Water, Peter," Jesus said, as if reiterating some unfinished explanation. "Water, the essence of life… life itself Peter." Jesus took both of Peter's hands into his, turned them, scanning, then abruptly released them, a satisfied smile taking over his face.

"Water is the essence of life, Peter. A marvelous substance, useful in many ways, capable of many forms. Men sweat water, men bleed water, men fish its seas. Water sustains life, quenches thirst, refreshes, cleans. Water gives life to men… yet water can also kill."

He paused, staring intently at Peter.

"Water is formless yet takes many forms. Its vessel defines its contours. Water has no color… yet is red when blood, blue when the sea, yellow when waste, white when snow. Water is liquid… yet can disappear into the air when near the fire and harden when high in the mountains. Water can be sticky and water can be evasive, slippery."

Jesus paused again, his eyes trained on Peter, intensifying, forming a hard squint.

"Water is all of these things, all of these forms and shapes, all of these colors, all of these properties… and yet it is none of these things. For these are just the many appearances of water. The appearance of water, while important, only defines water in its current context. Water, when experienced in its current context, is limiting. We can only experience the water as we see it, feel it, taste it. In a current context we focus on water as we sense it. The many other potentials of the water are difficult to recognize and easy to ignore… perhaps even to deny. Again, men experience water in a current context and it is that current context that defines a man's perception of water. That context is singular, immediate and sensory.

Yet every drop of water contains the potential — the essence — of all of its forms, all of its uses, all of its contexts. Water is not limited, in fact, is unlimited. The true value of the water, Peter, is its essence, its inherent potential, and not its current appearance."

Jesus gazed off, seemed distracted, then his features sharpened and he motioned for Peter to walk over to the rock that had rolled from his tomb. They were perhaps ten steps from his tomb now. Jesus sat down next to the rock cross-legged and gestured for Peter to do the same. A slight breeze twisted in blowing grains of sand off of the rock and into Peter's face. His fingers rubbed at the grit as Jesus gave him a smile of satisfaction.

"The wind, Peter... like the water... it cools us yet can hurt us. The wind is many things. Appearance. Context. Essence. Potential."

With that Jesus bowed his head and again uttered words that Peter could not understand. Peter felt a stream of air passing by his foot and blowing into the base of the rock. The stream intensified, a tiny but powerful pulsing, pushing away sand from in front of the rock, steady at first, then quickening. Peter instinctively rolled himself away from the air stream and jumped to his feet. Jesus said nothing, his focus on the rock silently instructing Peter to do likewise. Incredibly, the stream of air was sweeping away layers of the sand from in front of the rock, smoothly, evenly, rhythmically. Peter's lips parted involuntarily as he stared at the scene, transfixed. The trough in front of the rock widened and deepened in response to the steady stream. Then, gradually, evenly, the intensity of the air stream waned. Peter bent forward to get a closer view. The air had almost stopped now, blowing softly, single grains of sand wafting away from the base of the stone. Peter felt Jesus' presence standing next to him, both watching as the stone began to tilt forward, ever so slowly, then pitched itself into the trough, one final sway and gently to its new rest. Peter stayed silent for seconds then looked at Jesus catching his look of bemusement.

"The rock was on sand, Peter. Appearance. Essence. Tiny grains of sand have the essence to hold up big stones… but the wind has the essence to move sand."

For moments neither of them spoke. Peter could sense a brightening of the scene, the clouds that had interrupted the moonlight now were nowhere to be seen. Had Jesus control of the clouds as well?

"We need to talk about you, Peter"

The words struck at Peter sharply, his fright immediately renewed. His body responded with panic, his eyes wide, his face flushed, sweaty, his terror apparent. Was this to be his death? His appearance ripped back from him, his essence exposed?

Jesus sensed his distress yet was reluctant to calm him, wanted the full attention he would get from Peter's excitement.

"You denied me Peter. Three times…. Appearance?…. Or essence?"

Peter felt his terror subside and turn into a most unique

21

pain. He was a strong man, physically powerful, able to tolerate great distress. But no strength within him could spare him from this infliction, the confrontation with his greatest failure, the acknowledgement of his failure directly to the man who was his greatest influence. Peter turned to Jesus, his eyes searing with pain, felt himself somehow on his knees. And yet Peter felt himself begin to respond. How he had so wanted to make amends to Jesus, to apologize for his actions. How he had been tormented by the blunt reality that he would never get to do so. Now he had his chance, a chance to right things, to say what needed to be said, unconcerned with his impending fate.

"I failed you! I was so weak!" Peter felt his voice catch, felt words that he could not release, thoughts he could not organize and then, strangely, the beginnings of control. "I failed you," he said softly. I was arrogant in my strength; I could not see my frailty. I had doubts, yes I did… but I saw our triumph. Then… it didn't happen! Didn't happen as I thought. Not my way. Then they came… I panicked… you were gone… I saw them take you… saw…."

"You saw the appearance Peter…"

The words came quickly now, a flow of nervous release and confession. "I failed you though! Failed you in my one chance… when faith was required. When doubt needed to be overcome… when you needed me to be strong…." Peter paused, gasping, gulped a breath, looked up at Jesus, his eyes briny, glazed, his face awash, his voice near croaking, trying to shout, unsure, surreal.

"I failed you, I am so ashamed…. You are the Lord… my Lord… and my God! I am so heartily sorry… I beg your forgiveness, my Lord Jesus!"

With that Peter collapsed, prostrate, his face sideways in the sand, eyes closed, his hands extended, his energies utterly spent and his mind a blank. He lay there motionless, his body weightless yet unmovable, his mind gray. He felt an absence of time and a disconnect with his senses. He was aware of the grayness yet had no control over it. He felt himself receptive yet without stimulation; aware yet unknowing. There was complete silence. There was no movement. Only grayness.

He felt clean.

Peter lay in this state for some unknown time.

Gradually, Peter felt himself becoming more aware of his condition as if he were an observer of the gray and of himself yet still somehow within himself. An image began to form, slowly, swirling a bit, water, a boy, then sound, a splashing laughing combination, then a woman, the beginnings of focus. His mother! He recognized the boy as himself, remembered the day, joyful. Another image, his father, on a boat, lines wrapped around his forearm, smiling at him. More images now, snatches of remembrance, flowing into his consciousness, jumbled, out of sequence, playing with his brother, entering Jerusalem last week, pulling in fish, a child throwing grapes at birds, his mother again. Then a clear moment, sharp, framed in time and detail, the day he met Jesus.

The sea was rough that day and they could not go out.

They had fixed their lines, he and Andrew and Simon, and had some time. Some others were there as well. Someone suggested a race. Squat, stocky, block-like, he had never been a fast runner. He ran with them, tried his best and caught only ridicule for his results. He accepted their chiding at first then got annoyed. One comment finally put him over the edge. He glared at all of them, then picked up a rock the width of his shoulders, hunched into a squat and hurled the slab with an explosion of hip, shoulder, and grunt. He marked off the distance, scraped a line in the sand with his foot, came back, and proceeded to throw the slab a finger's length further. Then he dropped the rock at the starting point and glared at them all. Some tried, all failing, point made, Peter now "the Rock". Unseen, Jesus had watched from afar. When he approached the group Peter was in no mood for the stranger. But there was something about this man, something different, something about "fishing for men" and Peter decided to follow him.

More images now, flooding back, changing sequences, some repetitive, a replay of his denial, his wife's death, a childhood fight, the entry into Jerusalem again, dreams from his youth, cleaning fish, reaching into the tomb, confronting Jesus today. Peter could see the kaleidoscope of life events, see the part he played in each event, see with clear insight now what his motivations were, how pure was his heart. The results were not always pleasing as he could see behaviors that were not always honest or honorable. The clarity of his insights was disturbing to him, undeniable, raw, exposing.

His mind drifted through his life's events, some fresh and

distinct, others cloudy and long forgotten, all brought into new focus, all seen with sharpened insight. He catapulted through them, each bringing clarity to the "essence" of his being. He could not deny his motives when they were now clearly identified, could not deny his intent when his intentions were not admirable. And yet there were triumphs too, moments of goodness, of sincerity, moments of love. His mind began to accelerate now and Peter could peer into his being, the sum total of his work, separating now his "appearance" from his "essence". How good a man had he been? How had he treated others? How strong and how weak had he been? Peter could only observe himself now, view himself through a prism of pure honesty, the deeds done, his motives exposed, the impact of his actions indisputable. The recollections were rushing now, faster, blitzing by him, current, only days ago.

And then silence.

Utter and complete silence.

Peter realized that he was back in the present, his mind filled with adrenaline and completely alert. And yet strangely calm, a flat line of emotional response amid such an electric experience of awareness. He felt his mind becoming aware of his physical surroundings, the rocks and lights and shadows coming back into focus, moments passing. Then the voice and the unmistakable likeness of Jesus directly in front of him, his face emotionless and yet strangely transcendent.

"What is your essence Peter?"

Peter heard the words and immediately recognized the terrible weight of the question. He had been shown his essence, had seen his life in brutal honesty, layers pulled back, revealing, undeniable. So this was it, the terrifying nature of death, to have one's life revealed in truth, to be judged by one given true insight.

To have to judge oneself and determine one's own eternal salvation or eternal condemnation.

Peter considered the question, heard it again and again in his own mind, Jesus standing motionless in front of him, only an arm's length away, his appearance somewhat changed, human yet somehow not so. Then Peter began to feel a slight welling, sensed a certain life force flowing within him, an energy to his being, rushing through him now, a warmth literally running through his veins. He began to smile, could not compress it, his emotions roiling, a satisfaction and sense of happiness and peace washing over him like nothing he had ever experienced or imagined as he heard his own words.

"Yes… Yes, I have been a good man. I am deserving of eternal salvation."

With that Peter felt a concussive power in his head, a release of energy, a loss of vision and focus, the grayness back, as if he had suddenly stared into the sun. He felt himself struggle for his balance as his head began to clear. Before him stood Jesus, a smile of joy on his face, his veneer earthly and real. He moved forward and put both of his hands on Peter's shoulders.

"Blessed are you Peter, you have seen death."

Jesus released Peter, moved away, up the incline towards his tomb. Peter stood transfixed, the magnitude of his experience beginning to overwhelm him. He could feel the warmth anew, pulsing through him, moving his spirit. His mind was already reflecting on the experience, trying to dissect it and make sense of it when he was overcome with sheer happiness. The verdict — his verdict — was clear and true and inescapable. Forgive yourself Peter for you are saved!

Peter moved towards Jesus, his human emotions in full engagement, tears streaming down his face. Jesus sensed his approach, turned towards him, silent, smiling. Peter fell to his knees in front of Jesus, his head bowed, his voice choked.

"You are the Messiah, the Son of God, my Lord and my Savior, Jesus Christ!"

Long moments passed, time impossible to measure.

Peter remained sagging until Jesus put his hands under each of Peter's elbows and lifted him. Jesus looked Peter directly in the eye.

"I am the living God, Peter…Your faith has saved you," he said very softly.

More moments passed, surreal, and Jesus walked Peter up the incline to its top. Ahead of them lay the wide expanse containing Jerusalem, dark now but for sporadic fires, its blackness merging with that of the night sky, both sprinkled with similar lights, the horizon between the two melting and fuzzy. They stood side by side and Peter felt Jesus place an arm around his shoulder.

"There is much work to do, Peter. We must find the others. The word must be spread."

They stood silently, breathing in the cool air, the night

crystalline, fresh and clear, their eyes staring out over the panorama, their thoughts within themselves. Jesus broke the moment, turned and put both of his hands on Peter's shoulders, looked intensely into his eyes.

"You are the chosen one Peter. You are the strength... their strength... my strength. They look up to you. You will lead them. You are their rock... my rock as well."

Jesus spun around, looked out over Jerusalem, paused.

"You are the rock Peter... and upon this rock we will build the road to salvation and eternal life."

Peter felt his mind overwhelming itself, his thoughts flying, the magnitude of Jesus' pronouncement staggering him, could feel himself flushed and sweating... and yet strangely serene, resolute, at peace. Jesus gave Peter a moment then faced him, his lips forming a tight, full smile.

"There is much work to do... but first you must become clean." With that Jesus clasped Peter's hands, again murmured something unintelligible, and Peter's palms began to emit fat blobs of water, oozing. Peter cupped his hands, watched them fill, then tossed the contents over his face. Jesus broke into a full smile now, throaty with laughter.

"Water, Peter. The essence." He moved his head in front of Peter's face, smiling all the while, but his tone was firm and direct. "Water has many essences. If a man is wise enough to recognize them... and firm in his belief...

Jesus placed both of his hands, palms open, on the sides of Peter's face, his eyes hardening.

"... a man can walk on water."

Jesus looked skyward, muttered something, looked down at Peter and said,

"I am the living water Peter. Be clean."

With that, Peter's hands began to fill again, and he hurled the water up into his face and his hair, again and again, feeling the coolness run down his neck, along his hairline. He closed his eyes, drank for refreshment, his entire being soothed, bathing in this special peace. He hung his head, shook the water from his hair and face, rubbed his hands up and down his face one more time, then opened his eyes to the evening light.

He was alone.

CHAPTER 5

The road crested slightly, veering left, as he approached the familiar grove. He stepped off the path to the right and moved cautiously down the grassy incline, slick with the night's dew. His steps picked up momentum as he neared the bottom of the slope and he allowed the weight of his body to rush him forward the last few meters. Spread out before him was the olive garden. The trees rose up alternately thick then sparse in pattern with the rocky crags that dotted the landscape. The grove was flecked with shadows as clouds passed continuously before the high moon. The wind had picked up, the leaves rustling in a comforting cadence. He found himself smiling as he walked amidst the grove, over several gentle slopes, moving back into the area of older growth. The trees there had attained great height, perhaps 10 meters or more, with thick trunks covered with gnarled, scraggly bark. At a man's height the trees burst sideways into a complex and interconnected maze of boughs and branches, covered with grey green leaves. The harvest had left the ground carpeted with dead leaves and spoiled fruit.

Silently, the trees commanded their own sense of strength, of permanence, of perspective. Well over one hundred years old, these trees seemed to speak of other things, things more natural and timeless. The grove provided relief from harsh sun and cover from driving rains and yet the grove had always provided even more to Jesus. He had sought peace here in these groves, welcomed being alone here, contemplative, feeling the kindred connection. The grove had always seemed bigger at night, dark and foreboding yet with its own sense of envelopment. Jesus did not share that most unique of human fears — fear of the dark — and had, in fact, embraced the rich darkness of the grove.

He found the spot now, a slight clearing, sheaths of light popping onto the opening as the clouds moved past. He strode ahead perhaps ten steps, purposeful, bits of memories flashing, his emotions moving. Then he was there. He stood silently, staring down, the green area strewn with withered leaves and rotting fruit, the wind rolling the area, no signs showing from the anguish that he had experienced here only days ago. He felt bemused, a strange combination of disappointment and yet, surprisingly, undeniably, a sense of relief. He had had his moment here, so intense, so necessary, yet now completed, a memory, a relic of time, that most human of interventions. He dropped to his knees, surveyed a small circle of the ground, completely at peace. He picked up an olive and tossed it at one of the wide trunks nearby. Had it really happened? Had it only been days ago? He felt himself let out the deepest of breaths and the beginnings of a laugh. So strange, this human condition. He picked up another olive and flung it at the trees. Perhaps his garden friends could lend their perspective.

His had been a different transition. He had passed through the portal, had seen his life reflections similar to what he had allowed Peter to experience. But, for Jesus, the reflective process had been without insight. In his unique duality, he had known his mission, had known of certain outcomes in his life, the important ones pre-ordained. He had not lacked the penetrating wisdom — and subsequent judgment — that death offered men. What he had most experienced throughout his life was a separation from the Father, an angst that was never far from his consciousness and critical to the success of his mission. It was the pull of the Father, a pull towards the eternal, the drive to re-unite that constantly flowed through him. It was his mission to reflect that primal need to men, to show them that he was the vehicle by which men could satisfy their natural stirrings towards the Father. To be the way and the truth and the life for men. Still, his death allowed him to re-experience and re-visualize his earthly life before reuniting with the Father.

His difficulty lay in fulfilling this drive to reunite with the Father, experiencing the accompanying joy and fulfillment… and then again going through a process of separation from the Father. For all of his life Jesus had known about the flame of eternal life, had more knowledge and insight of the flame than any other human being, had passed through the portal of death to be engulfed in that flame, engulfed in its eternal presence… and now found himself being moved away from the flame, losing the flame, going backwards, towards separation again from the Father. Jesus had never had time to visualize what this phase of his assignment might entail, had not prepared for it, was not ready for the overpowering pull of the Father that he had so recently experienced. He had no guidelines for how to "go back". He was in a truly new phase of his existence, called to fulfill his final mission — the most important part of his mission — yet his spirit rebelled at his loss of the eternal. He had been "born again", returned to the earthly existence with all that that entailed, a return to a physical reality… and a return of the earthly yearn for the Father. He realized that his yearning, by nature of his duality, was more heightened, more intense than ever experienced by any man. His final mission would present him with challenges that were different from what he had previously encountered. Perhaps even more difficult.

Jesus stood up and immediately noticed his shadow. Seeing his shadow brought things into perspective. What was a shadow other than a recognition of distance and separation? The shadow reflects the appearance of the man but is not itself the essence of the man. Not even close. A shadow does reflect the vessel that contains the essence of a man but not always accurately — the further from the source of light, the longer the shadow; the closer to the source of light, the shorter the shadow. The shadow most accurately reflects the essence of the man as it nears its source of light until, eventually, ultimately, the light consumes the shadow. Becomes it. The shadow no longer seeks its source of light; it has become one with the light. No distance, no separation, no distinction between essence and appearance. Jesus was cognizant of these earthly realities and human motivations. How the Father had planned this! Create the light, be the source of the light, imbed a craving for the light into the human spirit, then let men seek the light and create ways to find it. And Jesus was to be the way.

Jesus noticed more shadowy movement at his feet and looked up into the spring sky. He could see clouds methodically moving, gently crossing the sky in a slow rhythmic cadence. Unhurried. Distance portraying their movement as a leisurely float. So strange, he thought, these concepts of time and distance. Distance from a source diffuses its light; distance from a source distorts its time relationship. Separation was the essence of the human condition; separation from the Father. Dilution by dimension. Jesus marveled at the incredibly simple juxtaposition of dimension. Time and distance created separation from the Father. As men are separated from the Father they face the challenge of connection back to the Father. Time and distance dilute a man's awareness, a man's longing, a man's focus. Man's innate longing for the Father was a matter of choice, of focus… and yet man possessed the freedom not to choose, not to focus, to ignore the longing… to drift. Men must be like beams of light, sharp and clear and pure. But separation from the Father allows a man to waiver, to lose clarity, to deny longing until a man floats like the clouds, serene but oblivious; adrift and unfocused. Death then brings to man its concussive implosion, a compressing, pell-mell race to the source, a laying bare of one's essence. Death brings the intersection of time and eternal presence, the horribly magnificent question, the profound magnitude of one's answer, all of a man's life reduced to the terrifying question, "What was your essence? Are you worthy of eternal life?"

But Jesus had come to bring a new order, a new reality. No longer would men await their light from distant and impersonal sources. No longer would men merely receive and reflect. No, instead men would initiate and seek. Through Jesus they would recognize their own light, a light from within, a light that would burst from the heart in search of its source. Their light would be different from that of the night stars, emanating from afar, from distant points. No, through Jesus, a man's light would be as though a beam had pushed through the earth's surface, thrusting upward, propelled toward its source, rising inexorably, a majestic assent in search of man's essence. So men would seek the Father and Jesus would be the conduit. This would be the new reality and Jesus would be the new light.

To teach men this had been his previous challenge. To demonstrate this now would be his supreme victory. Jesus' mission now was to reinforce, to clarify, to guide, to show himself to be the new light. He had completed half of his mission and the final task lay ahead. Yet Jesus was aware of a new difficulty. He was finding it incredibly hard to resist the pull back to the Father. He knew that he had to somehow reassert his humanity, to reconnect.

His thoughts turned to the one person he knew would be able to help him.

CHAPTER 6

He had walked for perhaps an hour, heading east, up into the hills, towards the emerging sun. The early shafts of light had begun to break the crest of the horizon, ever slightly, with hints of yellow and orange separating from the purplish ground. Jesus stepped off the path into the moist grasses, balanced on one leg, removed a sandal and swept his feet through the wetness to clean his foot. Then he repeated the movement, clapped the sandals together, let out a deep breath and continued. The path soon bore off to the left, towards the house that Joseph of Arimathea had found for the group, the trail familiar, and he could see the outline of the stone house up ahead maybe one hundred meters. Surprisingly, he noticed light at the back of the house, more than just a night lamp. He had not expected anyone to be awake yet let alone tending a kitchen fire. He neared the final pathway that led to the house, paused, deep in reflection, thinking that his timing was poor, that Mary was unlikely to be awake yet. He thought carefully about what he would say, how he would approach her. He stood motionless, tranquil, focusing, breathed in deeply, stepped over some rocky identifiers and slowly approached the house.

The house blocked any light. Jesus clung close to the house wall, his left hand lightly brushing the cold stone, as he carefully picked his way over the uneven ground, towards the rear of the house. As he neared the turn, he could sense activity near the fire, saw the movement of shadows, felt himself emerging into light. Clearly, someone was awake. He braced himself at the wall's edge, slipped his left hand around the turn of the wall, paused for a moment, then used his hand's leverage to pirouette himself into the open yard.

CHAPTER 7

She had awakened early, up for perhaps an hour already. Mary had slept fitfully the previous evening, her mind awash in images and recollections. Yesterday had been a swirl of events, more of Jesus' disciples finding their way to the house, meetings, recollections, fears, solemn tones and gestures, an intimidating visit from a Roman official, meals barely eaten, her attention drifting, dreamlike at times, the events of the previous day starting to become reality. She found herself most engaged when trying to calm others, could generate no enthusiasm for her own future, the events still too fresh to allow for perspective. James and Mary Magdalene had returned as promised. She could not help but notice the quiet sense of leadership emerging from her youngest son, already looking older to her. Joseph had been magnanimous throughout both to her and to the varied guests, hospitable, reverent, dignified. He had addressed the Roman official in measured tones, steely, as if ready to respond with hidden resources. Their meeting ended without incident and Mary felt comfortable that her presence would cause Joseph no further inconvenience.

There had still been no sign of Peter.

The morning darkness had been cool, a slight breeze coming off the hills, delightful and refreshing. Mary felt surprisingly vibrant, peaceful, at ease. Her immediate concerns about James had been alleviated as the officials had had ample opportunity to seize him and had chosen not to. She thought continuously of Jesus, already in the past tense. He had warned her of the danger, had implied his death was imminent, had seemed almost casual in his description, purposeful, unconcerned. She had lived with anxiety about Jesus' safety for three years now, saw firsthand the hostility that he could generate, and yet saw the genuine response of affection and hope that his mission had generated. She had comforted herself that the uneasy standoff with the Jews and the Romans could somehow be maintained despite the obvious antagonisms. While Mary had not always understood Jesus' message she could certainly attest to his resoluteness. He had foreshadowed his death to her yet she took no heed, her mind unwilling to fully contemplate such a reality. Her pain was still sharp, deep and piercing at his loss, yet she also found herself re-hearing other of his words, words about purpose, redemption... resurrection. She felt the small beginnings of acceptance, a resignation that her son's death would be like so much of his life, less than understandable to her, confusing, a function of this most unique of relationships to which she had agreed and to which she was a part.

Increasingly, her thoughts moved to Joseph, the images more vivid, the remembrances sharper, so long gone now, this most good-hearted of men, stoic, so accommodating of a relationship that he would never understand, his vow of acceptance to her, a simple, kind, determined man. He had never seen Jesus' work, had only faint hints of his ministry. Mary had always sought her peace from Joseph, his quiet strength. How she wished he could be here now with her, in close embrace, if only for a few moments.

A slight flash from the fire broke her reverie. Mary stepped over to the pile of firewood, inserted three solid pieces into the oven's retainer and instinctively blew into the opening. The flames sparked up instantly, peaking wisps of yellow and orange. On top of the oven, her sesame rolls were rising on the stone tablet, the air filling with their sweet smell. The rolls had always been a favorite of her family and it had seemed appropriate to her to make a large batch and bring them to the disciples gathered in Jerusalem. She scraped the golden rolls off of the tablet, stepped to her left, and placed them on the narrow wooden rack that sat on top of the side table. She turned back, pulled a large bowl towards her and re-mixed her batter. Then she re-oiled the tablet. Skillfully, she doled out equal measures of batter onto the stone, put her face over the heat, and breathed in deeply. She moved back to the rack, broke one of the smaller rolls in half, dipped it fully into the honey bowl, and twisted the roll until the honey coated it evenly. Then she spun the roll into the dish of sesame seeds and held it up for inspection. Delighted, she took a substantial bite, the honey and the seeds spreading out onto the corners of her mouth.

As she stooped for more fire wood she could see a long narrow shadow running in front of her, then past her, to her left. She saw the light robes, a hand emerging from a sleeve, reaching down to pick up a small piece of wood. Her fixation on the fire had left her slightly unfocused and she looked at the figure in front of her, blinking for clarity. Reflexively, she took the piece of wood extending from the figure's hand and turned back toward the fire.

"Thank you Joseph. I'm sorry if I woke you. I've been up for awhile…"

She began scraping more rolls from the stone, realized she had received no answer, and turned directly towards the figure. The light from the fire continued to distort the image and she squinted deeply. She recognized the familiar physique, the outline of dark, curled hair, the face beginning to emerge.

"Oh James!… You are early, my love… You must try one of these".

Mary reached for a roll, prepared its coating, humming a tune known only to herself, her smile brightening to full width. She turned back, extended the sweet roll, sensed fingers take hold of the roll but, further, felt a hand take hold of her wrist. She heard two deep nasally breaths, looked down at the hand, saw the rust-colored scab, her mind quickly freezing, an instant of fright. Her eyes lifted instinctively meeting his.

Jesus kept her hand firmly in his, felt her stiffen, fear engulfing her face. Her eyes were wide, rounded, brown, blank. He saw her throat move upward, heard it constrict, a slight chortle, a release of breath. He put down the roll and gently placed his other hand to her elbow, trying to help her fight through the moment. Her eyes stared into his, focusing, incredulous, and he could see her lips beginning to part. He could feel his own chest tightening, his throat drying, eyes beginning to fill, a shallow breath.

"Yes, it is me."

Her arms and shoulders reacted to the sound, her head turning slightly upward, and he could feel her push herself upright. He continued his grip, steadying her, her eyes locked on him trying to sort out realities. Jesus felt his own heart pounding now, emotion surging, took in a deep breath, tilted his head back, eyes closed, shoulders shrugging upwards, then released it, felt his chest lower, his chin following. Her eyes followed his movement, refocusing, blinking regularly.

"It is me," he whispered, his face softening.

Mary looked directly at him, swallowed gently, felt his hands move behind her, pulling gently, the feel of robes, warmth, the smell of manhood, felt herself releasing completely into his grip. His arms enveloped her now, chest to waist, her body weakening. She felt his face in her hair, felt his hand move behind her head, softly caressing then moving to her neck. Her eyes were closed now, unresisting, her consciousness beginning to swirl. A dream perhaps? How she hoped she could capture it then, so vivid, for replaying, a sweet remembrance of her son, so real she could even hear his voice. Thanks be to God!

For long moments they stood embraced, silent, both

hugging their dream. Jesus moved first, arched his shoulders back, separated from her slightly, looked onto her face. He caught the end of her smile, her eyes gently opening, moist, serene. He waited another full moment, tilted his head slightly, his lips beginning to part into his own smile. He could feel his eyes easing, his lips gaining momentum, unstoppable now, the smile beginning to overwhelm his face. She looked up at him, her mouth fully open, closed her eyes one more time, only a moment, and he felt her face drop against his chest. He heard her deep inhale, saw her hair move upward, then down again, her head warm and firm against him. His arms wrapped her tightly now and she responded in kind, her hands behind him, pressing his back in toward her. They remained in full embrace, moments passing, their breathing the only sound breaking the silence. Then Jesus adjusted his embrace and gently lifted her off her feet, up towards his face, their eyes level now, inches apart. He raised his chin slightly, closed his eyes, kissed her forehead, then gently let her slip to the ground.

They separated an arms length, both staring in wonderment at the other, neither speaking. Jesus lowered his head, looked down at his left hand, turned his palm upward, the deep purplish welt from the nail wound showing prominently. He stared at his hand, twitched his fingers, gently closed a fist, re-opened his hand and turned his eyes to Mary. She had followed his movements and had not yet looked up. Slowly, Jesus extended his open hand towards Mary. Staring at the hand, she reached across her body, wrapped his fingers into the palm of her left hand then gently rubbed her right forefinger over the wound, feeling the bumpy welt and prodding gently against the rusty scab. She began shaking her head, her eyes narrowing, memories beginning to flood her, as she placed her right hand completely over his. She pulled their joined hands to her face, rubbing them against her nose and mouth, then she turned her head slightly and brought the hands to her cheek. Her eyes were full and she could control her emotions no longer, her tears flowing, running down her cheek and onto the hands. Her shallow breathing intensified into deep nasal gasps, her throat constricting, swallowing, as she continued nuzzling their clasped hands.

Jesus could only watch, felt his human instincts flooding back into himself, triggered by this maternal contact, asserting themselves as primal, subduing the duality of his nature. He felt as if a different consciousness was spiraling into his being, a catalyst to his emotions and adrenaline, so real only days ago, then extinguished, hidden, now resurrected within himself. To this point he had felt almost an observer of himself, his first contact with Peter a shock to his system, his return surreal even to him, his feelings remote. He had felt the pang of desire, the constant tug of the eternal to which he had just been exposed, alternating in strength, pulling his mind away from this earthly return and directing it back to its ultimate place. Concentration was difficult, the pull of one consciousness against the other. Now this encounter, so real, so physical, an expression of the eternal love of a mother for her child. Jesus knew that he had truly returned.

Mary slowly separated herself from Jesus, each of her hands in his, their fingers entwined. She turned both of his hands upward, gazed upon the two fresh scars, and looked Jesus directly in the eyes.

"It really is you", she whispered.

Jesus let his hands go limp, completely in her control, his eyes warming, slightly crinkled, the smile breaking through again.

"Yes it is."

She pulled him forward, in full embrace against her, her strength surprising him, ran her hands along his back, smoothing his robes. She pushed back and moved her hands to the sides of his face, her fingers entwining his beard, paused slightly, then kissed his waiting lips. Maintaining her grip, she twisted his head slowly, lovingly.

"I didn't understand… I heard your words, heard what you said… but I didn't understand…"

Jesus put his hands on her shoulders, his dark eyes liquid brown, and his smile ebullient, his love for her pulsing through his body, radiating through his emotions.

"It is as it had to be… I am here now, Mother…"

Both pulled the other to them, simultaneously, and they locked in an embrace, Jesus with his arms around her neck and Mary's arms wrapped tightly around his waist. Minutes passed. Neither spoke. Now Jesus could feel a flow, a literal warmth that ran into and through his veins, a force of connectivity, an infusion of the life force he had known so well only days ago. Jesus felt himself physically begin to heat, his consciousness refocusing, sharper now, completely in the present moment.

Mary broke her grip and searched her oldest son's face. She opened her mouth to speak but could utter no words. She exhaled a long, drawn breath and Jesus could again feel her weight go limp. He moved her toward two chairs that were in some short grass just outside of the carpeted wall. She motioned for him to take one of the seats as she went back into the kitchen area. She returned momentarily, balancing a basket of the sesame rolls along with a plate of seeds and a bowl of honey, and placed them on the small table that was between the chairs. Mary caught Jesus' face, unmoving, his eyes wide, almost trance-like, lost in some special thought, staring out.

And then she felt it. A jolting stab of recognition pierced through her, a zap of heat, a searing new sense.

She was in the presence of God!

Mary fell forward hurriedly, her knees hitting the ground in an awkward position, nearly crossing. She lurched to her right then was able to balance herself, regain control, and bend forward until her forehead was near to hitting the ground.

"My Lord and My God", she blurted.

Jesus quickly rose from his chair and stooped down, put his hand under her chin, and gently lifted her to her feet. He shook his head, slowly at first, then vigorously, emphatically, his eyes closed and arched upward.

"No woman. It is I who honor you... Blessed are you among women... Please."

With that Jesus guided her by the elbow to her seat. Mary quickly regained her composure, anxiety flowing from her face. Jesus gave her a moment. Then he reached down for one of the sesame rolls, coated it with honey and seeds and took a large, aggressive bite. Excess seeds and honey formed at the corners as his mouth rolled the contents. He let out a loud guttural exhale, a half cough-half laugh, three more chews then he gave his mouth a full circular lick. His smile was contagious, his satisfaction so sensual and unabashed that Mary could only laugh herself.

"I always did love these," he exclaimed. Mary got up and poured them both a cup of water then returned to her seat, darted her fingers over the rolls, and picked out one of the smaller ones. She looked over at Jesus who was finishing the last of his roll, clearing the sweet mixture from his thumb and forefinger. Mary caught his eye, gave him a subtle, knowing wink, and gently bit off the tip.

Both of them settled back in their chairs, the night air washing over them, a cleansing coolness. Jesus got up and found a small blanket in the kitchen that he threw over his mother's lap. Mary pulled the blanket tight to her chin, brought her knees up close to her body so that the blanket would fully cover her. Jesus did just the opposite, extending his long, angular frame so that his legs were almost completely off of the chair. Each drifted peacefully, silently among their own thoughts.

"What will you do now? Mary asked quietly.

"I must gather the others… Peter will lead them… there is much to do."

"I must tell you that no one has seen Peter. James has been by with Mary Magdalene and I believe they are at another house that Joseph has secured. The authorities have been here but seem unconcerned. Joseph, no doubt, has settled things with them. I believe some of the others are still at the great house."

Jesus heard her words, snapped out of his reverie, returned to the moment. He leaned over towards Mary.

"I have seen Peter. At the tomb. He was searching… and now he has found."

The wind picked up, snapping through them, the wall carpet bending at its edge. Mary pushed up from her chair, threw the blanket around her shoulders, went into the kitchen, and found several decent size pieces of firewood. She carefully placed them over the ongoing fire, blew on them slightly, looked back… and saw two empty chairs.

CHAPTER 8

H e could see the early morning fires beginning to kindle, the city starting to awaken, jets of orange and yellow streaking up from the early horizon. As he descended into Jerusalem, Peter appreciated anew its enormous expanse, could see its outline coming to life in flickering bursts. The road evened and widened as he passed through the city's outskirts, groves at first then neighborhoods.

His plan was to head to their rendezvous house, the place where they had last gathered. Joseph had secured the house, a large, two-story dwelling with a great room on the second floor, and had ensured its safety with the locals. Despite their numbers, easily thirty or more, they had been innocuous to the neighbors, their celebration intense yet reserved, controlled. A number of them had bedded there — Simon, Andrew, Bartholomew, Martha, and Mary, others of the women — making arrangements and keeping security. Peter assumed that at least a few had remained or, if not, that the neighbors might know where they had gone.

He was close now, the house visible on the left, a dark square shadow framed against a rising hill. He could see the street beyond, the small public square, where they had seized Jesus, the ensuing chaos, where he had...

Peter turned the last corner, a stone's throw away. To his right Peter saw a blaze of light, two fires almost merged as one, flames splaying up from one of them. The smells reached him first, delicious, sensual, of bread and bird, pepper, saffron and tumeric, the lively smells of baking and roasting. Peter checked his pockets, felt the coins, and directly turned to the kiosk. As he neared the smells intensified, interspersed now with a controlled cacophony — birds squawking from cages, an oven hissing relief, flames sizzling from greasy drippings. He saw two men, the older one in back, anxiously working near the cages, animated gestures, the conversation inaudible but the tones apparent, loud, commanding, annoyed. The younger man — the son perhaps? — stood over the grill, meticulously turning the spits, the birds roasting evenly. He seemed oblivious to the older man, inattentive, head bent in concentration.

Peter took the last few steps and stood in front of the wooden money table. The younger man glanced up but quickly went back to turning three of the birds, grimacing as his forearm extended over the heat. The older man turned towards Peter, reached for a rag to wipe his hands, never interrupting the barking he directed at the younger man. As he neared Peter the light from the fire pit shown brightly on his face, a face engulfed in sweat, leathery, intense. Peter's attention had turned to the wares and he bent over slightly, breathing in the smell of the fresh warm bread. He moved his nose over to the roasted birds, the spicy aromas wafting up, his eyes half closed from the pleasure. Seconds passed. Peter looked up from the goods and met the older man's full, stern countenance. Neither spoke. Peter glanced off to his left, to the loaves of bread, and gestured, pointing three fingers in request.

The younger man now approached the table and laid five new birds on a rack.

"Very fresh", he said quietly, stating the obvious.

Peter picked up two of the sticks and twisted them slowly, admiringly. His eyes turned upward and met those of the younger man, whose tight smile reflected his satisfaction with his work. From the periphery Peter could feel the presence of the older man, unspeaking. Peter turned towards him and met a harsh, steely glare.

"You were with him", the man spit out.

Peter could feel his face flush, anxiety flowing upward, heating the sides of his neck, panic stabbing into his consciousness, his mind literally spinning as he fought to maintain control. He stared forward, past the two men, through them, unseeing, his eyes taking in shadows and fire and smoke, his lips drying, his body preparing for flight.

A long, full moment passed.

And then Peter began to feel it, slowly at first, his mind fighting back, recovering, the events of last night swirling, repeating themselves, Jesus, his words, his touch, Peter's epiphany, Jesus' soothing affirmation. It flowed now, continuous, pulsing through his thoughts, overwhelming courage manifesting itself throughout his body. Peter felt himself almost alone, in wonderment at his reactions, the sense of strength coursing throughout him, complete in his relief and calm.

He turned to the older man and eyed him directly, intensely, so much so that the man visibly blanched. Peter stared at the man, deeply, locked onto his eyes, then felt himself break into the beginnings of a smile. He exhaled deeply, never leaving the man's eyes, relief and confidence enveloping him.

"I am with him still."

The older man began to recover, the fear beginning to subside. He stepped back from Peter, feeling the need for separation. He remained silent.

"I am with him still," Peter repeated. "He is with us again, this day… I have seen him, spoken with him, touched him."

Peter turned suddenly and stared hard into the eyes and the face of the younger man.

"He is risen…" Peter whispered.

The older man began to retreat now, back to the cages, his confidence returning, his hand raised now, palm extended, gesturing, shouting something inaudible. Peter watched him return to his work, put down some coins, and picked up the loaves and the birds. His thoughts raced as he replayed the encounter, incredulous at his response, the strength flowing, a force like he had never encountered. He headed back into the street, towards the house, the sticks slung over his shoulder, the loaves under his arm, when he abruptly turned and looked back at the kiosk. He could see the younger man staring at him, transfixed, silhouetted against the fiery shadows.

* * *

A block away now and Peter could clearly see the light from the first floor fire. The barn door was open and he could see people stirring. Suddenly, he saw two figures leaving the barn area, two of the women, bustling forward heading up a parallel street back in the direction from which he had just come. They seemed to be in a hurry and the lead figure picked up her pace. He could hear their voices, agitated, but could not make out their words. Then the second woman began running and the first woman quickly followed.

CHAPTER 9

Martha had been up early, stoking fires, gathering eggs, preparing vegetables as the others began to stir. Mary had also been busy tending to the animals. They had remembered the words of Jesus and had planned their venture without advising the others. They placed spices and cloths in a basket and Martha led their way up the street.

"He said 'on the third day'. Is this the morning he meant?" Mary asked.

"I believe it is," Martha replied. "I wish we had left a little earlier... although there is no likely reason why the authorities would rush."

The morning sun was beginning to emerge and they could feel its early warmth. Full of excitement, they quickened their pace then began to run up the street heading towards the area of Jesus' burial.

* * *

Peter could only surmise their purpose, watched them disappear from sight, shrugged and took more steps towards the house. But he was troubled, unsure of what to do, curious about their actions. Was something further planned at the site of the tomb? Something Jesus had left unsaid? Or had communicated to the others? Something told him he should follow them and go back. Carrying the provisions, he tried as best he could to catch them.

CHAPTER 10

Peter did his best to keep the women in sight but they were determined, sprinting through the streets, stopping occasionally to keep their heading, out of the neighborhood, through the groves, the road gently starting its assent into the hills. They had slowed now and Peter was perhaps a hundred meters behind them. As they climbed, the women seemed to be disoriented, not quite sure in which direction to proceed. He was close to them now, nearing them as they faced each other in discussion about the proper direction. He could hear their voices clearly. It was Martha and Mary.

Peter knew they were close, only one quick turn, the tomb just on the other side of the incline that faced them. Martha sat on one of the larger rocks checking her basket and adjusting some of its content. Mary seemed distracted, faced away from Peter as if scanning the horizon as he approached them, only steps away now. Neither of them recognized Peter as his face was partially hidden by the loaves that he was balancing on his shoulder.

"It is just around this hill, follow the cleared path."

Martha and Mary looked at each other, curious to the stranger. Then Martha saw.

"Peter!" she blurted. Martha put down her basket and pushed hard off the rocks, racing to Peter, into his extended arms. He lifted her and swung her gently in a graceful circle. Now Mary was at his side and he bear hugged her to his chest. He carefully put the loaves and the birds onto a flat stone and wiped the sweat from his face onto the sleeve of his cloak.

"How did you find us?" Martha demanded, her face flushed with excitement. "Why are you here?"

Mary looked at Peter more solemnly. She hesitated then said, "They killed him you know. They crucified him two days ago. He was to be buried somewhere around here and we are trying to find his tomb. We came to tend him ."

Martha jumped in.

"We came to check on his words, 'In three days I will be risen from the dead'. It is the morning of the third day. We had to come… to check… and to see."

Peter kept silent, decided that leading them to the tomb would be the best approach. He moved ahead of them on the path. Martha followed, excitement in her step. But Mary held back, hesitant, her mind processing.

"Peter, how did you find us?… Why are you here?"

Peter's mind raced. What to say? How much to divulge? He was not sure himself why he had followed them. Why still had their paths even crossed? He chose silence.

"Come," he directed.

They made their way along the path then over strewn boulders, the surface rockier, up slightly, then over and down, through a small crevasse and, finally, to the open area. Peter could look across and see where he had entered only hours ago, could see the spot where he had encountered Jesus. Just ahead he could see the stone. He stopped, Martha at his side, as Mary took the last small jump down from a stone and joined them.

"It is just ahead," he motioned. Martha and Mary both stepped out ahead when Peter's conscience took hold of him.

"Wait!"

Peter cleared his throat and looked anxiously at the women. "He is not here"

"They've taken him!" cried Martha, her face grimacing. "I knew it!"

Peter felt his face go blank, unsure how to respond.

"How do you know this?" demanded Mary, her face a glare. Silence.

"Were you with them when they came?" she spat, her eyes narrowed now, menacing, accusing.

Peter felt his mind numbing, his senses retracting within. How to respond? His story seemed outrageous even to himself. And yet... and yet... hadn't Jesus appeared to him? Hadn't he felt him, heard him, talked to him? The watery hands, the stone moving, the experience of perfect insight, his judgment of salvation? The great request of him, the rock?

Peter reflected, a long instant passing. Then it began, a response. He could feel the force flow now, a gathering strength, pulsing through his mind and his body, taking control of his senses. The truth. The resurrection. The life. He could feel himself changing, his energies surging juxtaposed with an incredible sense of serenity and purpose. His mission.

Martha and Mary could see it too.

Peter looked directly at the women, his face relaxing into the beginnings of an understanding smile.

"I was here last night. I had to come... I had failed him. When I got here the tomb was empty. Like you, I feared the worst." Peter's voice trailed off and he tilted his head to the side, looking down. Then, abruptly, he snapped forward, eyes bright and intense,.

"Then he appeared to me... right over there... He took hold of me, looked into my eyes... I felt him... he spoke to me...."

His entire face was engaged now, fiery, a wild, controlled passion.

"Jesus is alive!... He is risen... As he said.... He is with us!"

Both women stood stunned, mouths slightly agape, the incredible words overwhelming them. Peter motioned for them to come forward and they walked the twenty paces or so to the tomb. Peter pointed out the stone and the indentation. Both Martha and Mary reached into the tomb then pulled back from it. Martha slowly sank to her knees. Mary stared at the tomb's opening, then, her senses sharpening, said quietly,

"We must hurry back and tell the others."

CHAPTER 11

Mary's encounter with Jesus had left her energized, adrenaline-filled, and further rest was out of the question. She finished another batch of sesame rolls, filled two baskets, left word of her intent with Joseph, and headed into Jerusalem to the meeting house. The sun had lifted just over the horizon, breaking brightly, the crisp spring air beginning to recede, replaced by a gentle warmth. Her mind raced with excitement, replaying her encounter with Jesus over and over, hearing the words, feeling his bodily presence, her mind oblivious to the passing details as she made her way to the house. She saw it up ahead now, one street away, could see activity, the kitchen fire visible, two men outside the barn door, other figures visible inside. She hesitated for a moment, instinctively glanced around, then walked briskly toward the men.

She was twenty paces away now and could see Andrew plainly, his tall appearance unmistakable. He was talking to Simon and appeared agitated, his voice low but his hands and face gesturing. He looked up, caught sight of her, looked past her, not recognizing, and continued his conversation. It was Simon who recognized her, raised his palm to Andrew, stopping the conversation, his mouth beginning to open. Andrew turned towards her as well. Mary stopped, put down her baskets, stared alternately at the two of them, her lips pursed but breaking into a smile. They seemed not to notice. Andrew moved first to embrace her.

"Mary, my word... It is so good to see you."

Simon now joined them, taking over her embrace, "Mary,... I am so sorry for your loss." He pulled her close, embraced her tightly, gave a kiss to her head.

She could see that Andrew's eyes were glazing with tears, his emotions asserting control of his face, his voice catching, needing to clear his throat. "Mary, I am so sorry... We didn't know what to do. We went to the house that Joseph had prepared... expected some kind of word... Peter wasn't... "

Simon jumped in, "No one knew the timing... we thought maybe they would remove him from the city, take him to the gate... that he would join us again..."

"That we would head west, toward the sea... away. James told us to stay, that he would get the details... Then we heard... it was too late." Andrew's sobbing was uncontrollable now and Mary could see that Simon's emotions were no better. Others heard the commotion, began to join them; Philip, Elizabeth, some of the daughters, all chattering, jostling to embrace her, talking over each other, through each other. Philip hugged Mary tightly, moved her to arms length, unable to speak, his eyes moist, throat gulping. John joined them now, moved through the group and reverently hugged Mary for a long moment. He seemed the most in control, looked over Mary's head, scanned the streets, motioned towards the large barn door.

"We should head inside."

Andrew held the door open and the group began moving through. Two of the children picked up the baskets and carried them inside. John continued to survey the streets, Simon joining him, a sense of anxiety beginning to assert itself. Mary stood motionless, momentarily forgotten, an amused look on her face. Then she stiffened, her face serious, eyes steeling a bit, soft yet piercing, alternating looks at the four men. They caught her silence, the change of mood, and halted. Their faces reflected a new apprehension. She must be here to announce something. What else could have happened? Some news of Peter? An aggrieved mother lashing out at them about their failure? Their courage? No, not James? Please no!

The group filtered back outside, into the street, forming a tense semi-circle around her. Mary stood stone faced, her eyes peering into the eyes of each person, her silence speaking volumes, as they braced for her announcement. Then, Mary's features began to soften, her eyes widening a bit, a glint of moisture, the corners of her mouth beginning to upturn. Still silent, the group began to pick up these cues, a couple of exhales, some slight smiles in response. Mary cleared her throat and her faced brightened unmistakably.

"He is alive. He is risen... He is alive!"

"Who's alive?" blurted Philip, only half hearing. "Peter?"

The cohesion of the group disintegrated into a cacophony of noisy inquisition, half thoughts, murmurs, quizzical gestures, uncomprehending. John tried to quiet them, raised both his arms over his head, palms motioning downward until he began to regain control over the group. John grasped both of Mary's hands, paused for a long moment to settle the group, then looked solemnly at Mary.

"Mary,… who is alive?"

"My son!" she shouted, exasperation beginning to show. Mary whirled towards them, their faces contorted, eyes squinting in confusion. Instantly, she recognized, then clarified for them.

"Jesus," she whispered. "Jesus… Jesus, he is alive!"

John let her words settle on the group, their murmurs rising in cross talk. John held up his hand to the group and they quieted. Always the analytical one, the pragmatist, he had heard the words and interpreted them to mean James. Now this stunning announcement. And yet Mary seemed so controlled, without hysteria, no hint of self-deception, of some illusory dream.

His mind processed quickly, as it always did, logically, deliberately.

"How do you know this Mary? Who told you?"

Mary looked at John, slightly impatient, caught herself, could see John's earnestness, realized the magnitude of what she had said, how it had been heard. She took in a deep breath, head tilted back then forward as she exhaled, straightened herself up and faced the incredulous group.

"He came to see me last night, at Joseph's house...
Jesus, I mean. Jesus came to see me; actually it was early
this morning. I was up, making these," she gestured down
towards the baskets " and he was there."

Her emotions raced as she recalled her own memories.
She fought for control, knew she must be clear, articulate the
news, the incredible message.

"I was at the oven making some rolls. I had been up early,
couldn't sleep... I saw this figure; I thought it was Joseph,
then James... He took the roll from me and looked at me...
I thought it was a dream... but he spoke to me. I touched
him... I held him, he held me...." Mary's voice broke and
her tears flowed openly. John moved to comfort her but she
gently extended her hand to push him away and continue.

"I touched him, held him in my arms... I felt the marks
from the nails, big purplish welts... Jesus is alive, he is with
us... he is risen!"

Mary could sense her faced was flush, taut with
emotion. She could see the shock on their faces, her words
overwhelming to them, unable to respond, transfixed. Andrew
moved towards her, a look of concern still evident.

"Where is he now?"

"I don't know... He left as I turned my attention to the
oven."

Andrew caught John's reaction, ever slight, their eyes
locking. A powerful dream perhaps? A cruel hoax of the mind
preying on a grieving mother? A sedative from Joseph?

"Come inside Mary," John said soothingly. "Come in

and rest… and eat. It sounds like you have had an incredible night." Elizabeth and the other women took Mary upstairs, past their quarters, to the great room. John backed off from the group and returned to the barn door, to where Andrew and Simon were whispering.

"I don't know what to make of it," John quietly declared, responding to the unasked question. He turned towards Andrew; their faces mirror reflections of the same inquiry. "Could it really be?"

Simon took a step back from the open door, tugged on Andrew's sleeve, and motioned for him to come forward. The men looked up the inclined street and could make out the figures of Martha and Mary returning. The third figure looked unmistakably familiar.

CHAPTER 12

Martha saw the group gathered outside the barn door and could contain herself no longer, impulsively running ahead and shouting the news. Mary and Peter lagged behind carrying Peter's provisions. As they neared, some of the women came out to meet them taking the provisions from them, the crowd swelling into the barn. But John held back as did Simon. Peter caught their looks, braced for the moment, knew that he must face their scrutiny. Some had witnessed Peter's failure; all had heard of it. Now he must address their hurt, their scorn, their questioning.

All were silent. John and Simon shifted their weight nervously, looking toward Peter but past him, none of them knowing how to start. Finally, Peter made a deep clearing of his throat, pushed his left hand into his eye, rubbing and pushing against himself, mouth slightly scrunched and eyes squinted.

"I have seen him... It is true."

They looked at Peter, unspeaking, anxious for more.

"I went to the tomb last night... trying to connect. Trying to reconcile... somehow. I went to the tomb and he was not there. Then... then he was with me, completely real. Alive!

Talking, breathing, warm… as I am before you."

John cleared his throat, about to speak, but Peter held up his hand.

"I know I failed you… I failed myself, failed him. But, as I stand here before you… he forgave me… made me forgive myself." Peter's eyes moistened over and he fought for control.

"He talked of our work… of what we must do."

Peter took in a deep breath, his thoughts jumbled, waiting for order and clarity. Then a muffled noise to the side. Simon turned first. There in the barn doorway stood Andrew guiding Mary by her elbow.

Mary's eyes locked onto Peter as she stepped forward to embrace him. She stopped inches from his face and placed her hands to the side of his beard.

"You have seen him too," she said quietly, more affirmation than question.

Peter put his hands to her head, met her eyes, both of them teary, sharing this most unique of bonds.

"I saw him at the tomb… last night," he closed his eyes and began shaking his head back and forth, "It's incredible…."

With that Mary wrapped both of her arms around him, spun him towards the barn opening, and began walking inside, raptly attentive to him, oblivious to all else.

Andrew, Simon, and John watched them until they were out of sight. They looked at each other silently, unsure of how to interpret what they had just witnessed. Simon and John moved to follow them.

"Can it really be?" Andrew said to no one.

CHAPTER 13

As they ascended the steps to the great room on the second floor they could hear the buzz of noise, the fragments of conversation, the excitable energy that Mary and Peter were generating. They stood with arms linked, Mary beaming her brilliant smile, the rest of the disciples, the women, the children automatically moving across from them to the other side of the room. Mary caught sight of Andrew, Simon and John entering and waited for them to find a place.

"We have both seen Jesus," she said calmly.

"He is alive. He is real," Peter asserted, "He is with us... He is risen!"

A palpable murmur rose up, faces turning towards each other, mouths open, simple expressions of awe. Mary scanned them, caught faces individually, focused her smile on them, gently shaking her head in wonderment.

Peter stepped forward to the middle of the room.

"He said there is much work for us to do. We must make ourselves ready."

From the back corner a slight commotion stirred, the sound

of voices moving up the stairs, the grunts of men carrying heavy loads. The first of the men came through the door, back to the crowd, barking directions to two of the men that were still below on the steps, a man of medium build with thick yellow-brown hair, carrying a large sack filled with bread.

It was Thomas.

He spun slowly towards the center of the room, facing the crowd, a commanding presence, the voice rich and deep. His face was awash with sweat from the exertion, wetness also streaking through his hair, rivulets down his neck. His eyes met Peter's, not recognizing at first, blank. As he realized it was Peter, his face could not contain his emotions, a look of scorn blanching it, his eyes glimmering disdain.

"Ah, the Rock," he said dismissively, his tone even and controlled, barely above a whisper.

He turned his back to Peter, said a few inaudible words, reached for a hand towel and began wiping his forehead then his neck. Peter stood in the middle of the room in awkward silence, tension beginning to roll over the room, through the crowd. Mary moved a step closer to him.

Thomas took a long moment wiping his face again, back still to Peter, the silence overwhelming. Finally, Thomas turned to Peter, his face a deep red, his eyes filling with intense rage. He gulped once, saying nothing, his eyes never leaving Peter's. In full glare, Thomas picked up a pear and took a large, crunchy bite, breaking the deafening silence.

"Nice of you to join us," he spat out, chewing loudly, still glaring.

Peter let a long moment pass by. His voice was calm and earnest.

"We have seen Jesus... He is alive, Thomas... He is risen from the dead!"

Thomas looked at Peter and then let out the longest of exhales, slow, deliberate, releasing, his anger beginning to subside, overcome by the events, the circumstances of the last few days, unable to process anything more, unable to comprehend, at his end.

"I'm just trying to get us all bread," he murmured, shaking his head in bewilderment.

"Thomas... he is risen. He is alive... He appeared..."

Peter's voice was halted by the sharp rap of Thomas' hand as he slammed it against the table.

"Enough!... Enough of this!"

"Jesus is alive," Peter began again, slowly, calmly.

Thomas could bear no more. He turned his back to Peter, placed both palms down on the table, bent low, then pushed himself up hard and whirled around to confront Peter. His voice was loud now, animated, filled with passion,

"I will believe it when I see it! Unlike you...." He paused, deliberately, dramatically, head involuntarily nodding up and down, faced flush, "some of us were there. We saw the nails, saw the blood. We saw the lance... We saw, Peter!"

This release of emotion seemed to comfort Thomas, words that had built up, seethed inside him, given their vent now. Thomas took a sidestep back to the table, searched for his pear, remarkably controlled now. He turned back to Peter, his face drained of passion, a certain look of resignation. His voice was controlled now, almost matter-of-fact,

"I'll believe he is alive when I can see him myself. When I can put my fingers into the nail holes and the side slash."

He paused, looked to his right, catching sight of some of the disciples, all staring at him, some nodding gently. He turned back to Peter, finally becoming aware of Mary's presence, nodded to her, waited a moment, then restated calmly,

"That is when I will believe."

A stunning silence filled the large room. Even the most forceful of the group — John, Simon, Mary — were incapable of mitigating such a bold challenge. Despite the assurances of Mary and Peter, some clearly were skeptical. Perhaps it had all been a noble cause now gone bad. Perhaps they had deceived themselves, been mislead, had misunderstood. And yet they all knew Mary, knew Peter, knew them to be stalwart, trustworthy. Many took heart in their assurance that they had seen Jesus. Still the nagging perception existed that the two people most certain of having seen Jesus were the two people who might be the most susceptible to a vision. Who might have the most need to experience such a vision. Perhaps Thomas spoke for many in articulating their innermost doubt.

Mary and Peter remained in the center of the room, having borne Thomas' brunt. Remarkably, they seemed somewhat oblivious to the sense of awkwardness that was settling throughout the room, almost as if floating above it. Mary was about to speak when the group's attention turned to the top of the stairs. She could see James and Mary Magdalene

71

leading a group into the room, spilling over to the side toward a window, Philip and Bartholomew and Judas, and some of the wives. The room was becoming very crowded, confined in space as well as spirit. The air was warming and some of the group began to fan themselves.

A couple of the men gathered around Thomas who looked disheartened, dejected. They whispered in low murmurs. Mary cleared her throat and the group's attention immediately centered on her. She had known all of them, many since the beginning, and had a respect and stature among them, a certain commanding presence. She scanned the room, squinting a bit to focus on some of the individuals, then her face relaxed, looking more over them than at them.

"We have seen him… Peter and I… He is alive." She reasserted.

Silence hung over the room. Individuals began talking amongst themselves, searching looks, some gently shaking their heads, others staring straight ahead, alone in their thoughts. James broke the silence.

"There are fresh provisions downstairs. Bread and meat and fruit."

The group began to move to the stairs, slowly, deliberately, snatches of conversation, low tones. James, Mary Magdalene, Bartholomew and Judas all rushed to Mary and Peter, their voices animated and inquisitive. James hugged his mother lovingly, kissed her forehead, then stepped past her and gave Peter a long, full embrace. The others did likewise, relieved to see him safe and well. The group drifted towards the corner of the room where a large table held jars of water and wine. Mary and Peter tried to explain what had just occurred but were summarily halted by James.

"You just said that you saw him, that he is alive... Both of you have seen him?"

"Yes," Peter responded immediately. "He is alive. I saw him last night, your mother saw him this morning... He is alive."

"James, your brother is alive! We spoke to him, heard him... I held him... felt his hands." She looked at her son, her face reflecting awe, incredulous.

Peter looked hard at James then moved his focus to Judas and Bartholomew and Philip.

"There is disbelief in this room," was all he could say.

They poured themselves drinks and continued conversing as the crowd began making its way back into the room, to their chairs, others seated on the floor, backs against the wall. The air quickly began to warm and stale. Peter and Mary moved back to the center of the room, James and Mary Magdalene joining them. The crowd's attention focused on them, uncertain, anxious.

"My brothers and sisters, we have been through much together," Peter started boldly. He scanned the crowd moving his focus right to left. "But we know that there is disbelief in this room... disbelief amongst us..." Peter stopped abruptly, in mid speech, mid word, as his scan went all the way left to the table of water and wine. There stood a tall figure, clothed in white, about to pour some wine into a cup.

There stood Jesus.

Peter's look went incredulous, others picking up on it, their attention turned towards the table. Some glanced over at the stranger, unseeing, and turned their attention back to Peter. Others saw immediately, their gasps audible, reflexive cries, some unmistakably fearful, terrified. The room electrified.

Jesus did not look up, finished pouring his wine, then straightened and turned to face the group. He looked impassive, his face blank and focused, and he stepped towards the party in the middle of the room. He went to his mother first, put his wine goblet down on a table, and hugged her, a long reverent embrace, then kissed her on the top of her head, smelling her hair. He turned to James, his face relaxed, eyes soft, his face unable to contain his smile. He took his younger brother into his arms, caught a look from James' watering eyes, whispered something privately to him, then both bear hugged each other. He released James, his face completely beaming now, moved to Mary Magdalene, again whispered something privately to her, both breaking into a quick laugh, she beginning to cry uncontrollably.

Jesus faced Peter, moved him a few steps away from the group, the two of them together now. Peter's eyes were very wet but he maintained control, powered by some internal force, accepted Jesus' bear hug. Jesus pulled his face away, looked serene, and said something privately to Peter. Peter closed his eyes, nodded affirmatively several times, re-opened his eyes and broke into an overwhelming smile.

Then Jesus turned Peter by the shoulder to face the group sitting at the main table. He moved next to Peter's side, put his arm around Peter's shoulder and gave Peter a squeeze. On Jesus' face was an indescribable look of complete triumph.

The room erupted in emotion, everyone crying, hugging, looks of disbelief and wonder, their attentions alternating between each other then back to the main party in the middle of the room. Jesus said nothing, let the moments transpire, his face frozen in smile, in private contemplation, Peter at his side, surveying the group.

Jesus let the din continue then raised his hand. At last Jesus spoke.

"Peace be with you," he said simply.

Upon hearing his voice, many in the group lapsed back into tears, the reality overcoming them; others were joyous, bursting into laughter. Again, Jesus let the crowd's reactions take their course then again raised his hand for silence, his face serious.

"Peace be with you... I am with you again today. I am the resurrection and the life. I am the way... and the truth... and the life." His voice was commanding, authoritative. He let the group react to his words, tilted his head back, his jaw slightly forward, and allowed himself to break into a smile. He seemed greatly relieved.

"Peace be with you," he repeated in a hushed tone.

The room stayed silent, pregnant with anticipation.

"Thomas" Jesus commanded.

The gasp in the room was frightening. Terrifying. Hands went to mouths, eyes widened, some of the women began crying softly.

Thomas stepped forward, his face awash in sweat, eyes circular, his fear palpable, surreal. He moved forward slowly, hesitant, almost measuring his steps, awaiting some form of unimaginable fate. Jesus said nothing and his face gave no indication of his mood or his plan of action. His eyes squinted a bit and bore into Thomas as he made his last final approach. Thomas could barely control himself, gulped repeatedly, his eyes pouring out tears, rivulets running down his cheeks.

Jesus gave Thomas one final stare. Then Jesus' jaw relaxed and his lips curled up at the corners into the beginnings of a slight smile.

"Peace be with you Thomas," he said quietly, breaking the tension.

Thomas' head began to shake as he bit hard into his lip trying desperately to maintain control.

Jesus said nothing, allowing the moment to complete itself. The room was without sound, spellbound.

Jesus looked down at his right hand, the purplish welt of the nail hole clearly visible to all. Very slowly, reverently, he extended the hand towards Thomas, palm up. Then, with his left hand, took hold of Thomas's right hand and guided it towards his palm. He moved Thomas's forefinger to the wound and gently pressed it against the scar. He looked Thomas deeply in the eyes, saying nothing. Thomas felt the wound, frozen in his fear. Next Jesus took his right hand away and used it to lift the side of his cloak exposing an angry yellow black bruise encasing a purplish slice of scar. Jesus took Thomas's hand and moved it toward the wound as Thomas began to lose all semblance of control, his body convulsing, eyes overwhelmed with tears, his hands trembling. Jesus purposefully guided Thomas's hand to the wound then released his grip and allowed Thomas to probe the wound on his own.

Thomas looked up at Jesus, completely overcome, sank to his knees, his voice a croak.

"My Lord and my God."

Thomas was crying uncontrollably now, on his knees, his fingers still against Jesus' side. Likewise, virtually everyone was in tears, stunned into silence, sharing the pain and the awe of the moment, identifying their innermost feelings with those of Thomas. Jesus looked across the group, caught some of their faces, then turned towards his mother and Peter. Mary's face was frozen in sympathetic pain for Thomas. Peter looked blank. Mary Magdalene was crying and James had his arm around her, whispering some comfort.

Jesus let the silence evaporate into the group until he had their complete focus. He took Thomas by each of his hands and lifted him to his feet. He measured his words and addressed Thomas all the while looking past Thomas and focusing his gaze onto the crowd.

"Blessed are you Thomas for having seen and believed. Many will be called to believe without seeing."

Jesus let those words sink in to the group. Then he wrapped his arms around Thomas, spoke something in his ear, and walked him over to the table to his seat.

Amidst a penetrating silence Jesus walked back to the

center of the room, near to Peter. He reached past Mary to the table, picked up his wine, and sipped twice. Mary caught his eye briefly and then moved towards him, a mother's instinctive support. Jesus cleared his throat, looked over the crowd, glanced over at Peter and made a slight gesture towards him.

"This is Peter, the rock upon which we will build our church."

Peter had a serene look on his face, a unique mixture of intensity and relaxed confidence. He took Jesus' hands into his own, looked directly at Jesus and nodded his head affirmatively, accepting the hallowed assignment. Jesus' face broke into a broad smile. He kept Peter's hands in his for a long moment then looked out at the crowd, making a quick hand gesture for them to rise to their feet. They rose and stood as one, some instinctively holding hands, some of the men placing their hands on the shoulders of their wives, others with their arm around the shoulder or waist of whoever was next to them. Jesus advanced a step ahead of Peter and looked around the room making eye contact with each one of them. A certain momentum was building now, a force, and they could all feel it, a sense of communal well being, an intensity of purpose to which they were all committing, a feeling that had its origin at their last supper and now was manifesting itself throughout their collective entity. The incredible feeling of being in the presence of God, frightening, and yet so naturally comfortable. As had happened just days ago, an invincible feeling of magnificent purpose descended on each of them.

They were looking at each other, those next to them and those across the room, smiles overtaking their faces, nods of acknowledgement to each other, a need for physical contact. The air in the room had taken on a warmth that could not be described, a unique sense of comfort and security permeating the room, a special form of energy emanating from Jesus and enveloping them.

A holy spirit.

Time stood still for them, irrelevant now.

Finally, Jesus broke the spell.

"My peace I give you... I am the resurrection and the life. The Father has delivered you a Savior. You must go and spread this good news... I promise you, wherever two or more of you are gathered, I will be with you in this spirit."

CHAPTER 14

The crowds had grown thick, larger by the day, more and more people joining them as the news of Jesus spread. They were on the main road out of Jerusalem again, Peter leading them, heading towards the open knoll with its surrounding rocky formation. The semi-circular arrangement worked well for them, the day's speakers able to ascend the rocks and preach out to the large numbers spread across the grasses. Andrew and Simon were in a middle group and had the best sense of the multitude that accompanied them. Andrew, being tall, could scan the crowds in every direction and thought this day's numbers were by far their biggest. He joked with Simon that if they could spread all of the followers on the road in a single file then the line might extend all the way to Phrygia.

As was his want, Jesus appeared sporadically. Some days he accompanied them for virtually the entire day, fully engaged, preaching and reaching out to the crowds. On other days he was less visible, less active, almost an observer, perhaps just interacting with select individuals and then only for a moment. Peter had clearly asserted himself as their leader, directing activities, his personality forceful and dominant. Other of the disciples and the women had assumed various responsibilities for logistics and coordination. Peter tried to gather the group each night but already it was becoming apparent that the size of the movement required that he assign responsibilities to the disciples and let them minister as they saw fit.

On this day, Andrew and Simon walked amidst the crowds, feeling the surging energy of the multitudes. Today, Jesus walked with them as well and, as was his habit, said very little. Increasingly, Jesus was deferential to the disciples, particularly to Peter, a watchful observer, almost as if a proud father to his newly independent son.

The crowd began to slow, bunching up and halting in response to a disturbance. Andrew, Simon and Jesus made their way forward, through the stalled crowd. Up ahead, to the side of the road, they could see the problem. A family had taken a position just off the road waiting for Jesus to pass. Word had spread that Jesus was approaching and now the oldest son, a young teenager, was leading his father, hand in hand, tugging him forward to the edge of the road. Just in their wake were the man's wife and the rest of his family, two younger daughters and two very young sons. The man's head was tilted skyward and he was shaking it from side to side, mumbling something unintelligible. He was clearly blind. The teenage son caught sight of Jesus as he approached and exhorted his father to move faster.

Jesus came upon the boy and his father and said nothing,

a stern look on his face. Andrew and Simon had both held back slightly letting Jesus advance. They could not quite hear the conversation as Jesus first asked the boy a question then another to the father. They could see Jesus squat down and spit into the dirt, the beginnings of his familiar antidote. Then Jesus abruptly looked up as a ball rolled by him, a simple child's toy, hide and sand and feather. Still stooping, Jesus picked the ball up. One of the family's youngest boys immediately appeared in search and stopped directly in front of Jesus. They were at eye level to each other. Jesus said something to the boy, inaudible to them, then rose to his feet, his face in full smile, laughter erupting. He motioned for the boy to run and then reached back and tossed the ball towards him. Another laugh and a shout to the boy that they could not hear. Then, Jesus turned back towards Andrew and Simon, the laughter draining from his face, mouth slightly agape, half smiling, an imploring look directed at them, his eyes locked on them.

A long silent moment passed. Shockingly, Jesus looked away and walked off to follow the boy.

The teenager took a step towards Jesus, began to shout after him but could get out no words. Andrew and Simon looked at each other, knowing but apprehensive, accepting their silent assignment. Andrew moved first, found the spit, added some of his own, mixed the muddy gruel and placed a large dab on his forefinger. He looked once more at Simon then took the leap of faith.

"What would you have us do?" he asked the father.

"I want to see! I believe you are the Son of God... Jesus. Please, I ask you... please let me see!"

Andrew squared up with Simon who had also reached down to pick up some of the mud. Simon looked at Andrew, closed his eyes and said in a whisper,

"Lord, I am not worthy to receive you. Only say the word and I shall be healed."

With that Simon dabbed the man's left eye with the mud while Andrew did the same to his right eye. The man reacted to the contact, recoiled slightly, rubbed his eyes to clean away the substance, and began blinking furiously.

The crowd had circled them, absolutely silent.

After a moment the father turned to his son, lifted his hand and touched the boy's face, running it along the side of the boy's features. His eyes were opened completely wide. Slowly, he began to drop his eyelids to their normal position and, as they lowered, the man's face burst with emotion and astonishment.

"I can see! ...I CAN SEE!!!"

His wife and children rushed to join him, all attaching themselves, all hugging him. He checked each one of them, just as he had the teenager, running his hands over their features, his voice slowing, down to a trembling whisper,

"I can see... I can see."

Andrew and Simon could only stare at each other, incredulous at what they had just done. The front observers in the crowd erupted in reaction, some falling to their knees, others shouting of the miracle they had just observed. News of the healing rippled through the crowd, a wave of noise and motion.

Andrew felt himself draining, could not speak. He put a hand to his forehead and looked down, trying to comprehend. Simon glanced once more at Andrew, peered down again to the muddy spot, then burst into tearful laughter.

CHAPTER 15

The winter winds whipped past him, snapping plumes of beige, smoky sand, white wisps alternately cracking across the road then swirling directly into his face. He had been on the road since early morning, passing travelers, merchants, pilgrims, carts and asses and dogs, all similarly bent forward, heads down, necks contracting into their bodies. The wind enveloped him, its special whistling forming a unique insulation. Physically, one could only push forward; mentally, one could only seek refuge in deep thought.

It had been high noon when he had passed the last oasis and his throat had become gritty with thirst. It was beyond mid-afternoon when he could see the first towers, the dark shadows of buildings beginning to form below the temple identifiers. He was close now and his mind began to re-engage, contemplating the task ahead. He put down the small satchel he was carrying and adjusted his scarf, a jolt of cold on his neck, invigorating him, his enthusiasm heightening. On his back he carried a larger satchel that was filled with various parchments and scrolls and writing utensils. He had planned this trip for months.

He walked by a small outpost just outside the city gates, a tiny hut and a stall of goats with several dogs keeping watch. He was tempted to enter the hut, could see gray smoke twisting violently upward, thought of the warmth and provisions there. But he pressed on. The road crested and then he was on the decline, the wind lifting him forward, toward the gates. The gates were formidable, heavy wooden panels, braced open, and he passed through without incident, the wind dampening any interest the guards had in their appointed task. One guard was seated in semi-seclusion just inside the gate, away from the elements, and he seemed to be in charge. He addressed the guard, made his request, produced him two coins, re-adjusted his satchel straps, and hurried across a small courtyard. He was close.

He pushed through two narrow streets, dense with merchants and food kiosks, the sweet smells from the food and the fires reminding him of the journey's difficulties. He ignored the squawking appeals of the vendors and broke off to the right into a more open expanse. He could see the house now just as the guard had described it, a low, stone building, open in the middle, a distinctive rock formation in the front. Red carpets covered much of the opening just as he had been told. A gray pallor hung over everything, the winter dusk beginning to descend.

As he pushed forward he noticed movement to his left out on the periphery. Walking toward him was a woman, head down and heavily scarved, carrying a small satchel and a water jug that appeared to be quite full. He watched as she put down the jug, adjusted her grip, and hoisted it unevenly.

As he neared her he could see that she was quite old. Once again she placed the water jug down, hunched over it, her hands working the handles, oblivious to his presence.

"Woman, may I help you with that?" he shouted into the wind.

She looked up, surprised, nodded her head in the direction of the jar's handles, a silent request for him to lift. They both lifted the jar centering it between them. She looked directly into his face, her olive brown eyes alive, vibrant, her face furrowed deeply, a smile, and a nod of silent thanks. She motioned again, nodding toward the stone house, indicating her destination. Immediately he released his grip and the jar thudded into the dirt.

"I am looking for the woman they call Mary Magdalene."

She looked at him, eyes perching upward, brightening, a tight lipped smile spreading across her face.

"Well you have found her," she replied, slightly bemused.

The wind had lessened, easing a bit, making conversation easier. She released her scarf and it gently fell to her shoulders revealing a thick bun of gray hair. Petite in stature, she eyed him serenely, her face seeming to anticipate a serious question or request.

"My name is John. I am so glad to have found you. I have come a long way to meet with you. I am trying to write about the events that took place here… Jesus and all. I understand you were with him. I was hoping I could talk to you about him."

She looked at him in full smile then turned her eyes away, her thoughts going private, her face turning whimsical.

"Come," she said, motioning towards the house and lifting one of the handles. He could not contain his excitement as they approached the dwelling.

"Are there any others still around… that I might speak to?"

Mary Magdalene did not reply. As they took their final steps one of the curtains was pulled back and an elderly man came out to meet them. Gray haired, hatless, slightly stooped, he seemed a spry and energetic man. He bounded over to Mary Magdalene, kissed her cheek, took the handle from her, and nodded thanks to the stranger. Then he looked back at her and she motioned them all inside.

There were two chairs positioned by an open fire. The elderly man found a third chair, spread them in a new formation and they all sat down. Mary Magdalene poured them drinks and introduced the stranger.

"This is John… He has come to talk to us about Jesus. About the events."

Gesturing to the elderly man, Mary Magdalene turned to John and said, "This is my husband James… Jesus was his brother."

James looked at Mary Magdalene, his eyes wide and warm. Then he turned towards John, adjusted himself in his chair, crossed his legs, ran his hand through his thin shock of hair and tilted back slightly.

"We have much to talk about."

Printed in the United States
84079LV00002B/24/A